Been There!
CHINA

Annabel Savery

W

F

Facts about China

Population: 1.3 billion

Capital city: Beijing

Currency: Renminbi yuan (RMB, ¥)

Main language: Mandarin Chinese

Rivers: Yangtze River, Yellow River, Pearl River

Area: 9, 596, 960 square kilometres (3, 705, 406 square miles)

An Appleseed Editions book

Paperback edition 2014

First published in 2011 by Franklin Watts
338 Euston Road, London NW1 3BH

Franklin Watts Australia
Level 17/207 Kent St, Sydney, NSW 2000

© 2011 Appleseed Editions

Created by Appleseed Editions Ltd,
Well House, Friars Hill, Guestling, East Sussex TN35 4ET

Planning and production by Discovery Books Limited
www.discoverybooks.net
Designed by Ian Winton
Edited by Annabel Savery
Map artwork by Stefan Chabluk

ISBN 978 1 4451 3285 3

Dewey Classification: 951'.06

A CIP catalogue for this book is available from the British Library.

Picture Credits: Alamy: p5 bottom, p8 (An Qi), p17 (Robert Fried); Corbis: p15 top (Michael Christopher Brown), p16 (Jose Fuste Raga); Discovery Photo Library: p7 top (Chris Fairclough), p24 (EASI-Images/Adrian Cooper); Getty: title page & p26 (Bruno Morandi), p5 top (James Nelson), p7 bottom (Tim Graham), p20 (Keren Su), p21 (Nicholas Pitt), p22 (Yann Layma), p25 (Keren Su); Shutterstock: p2, p6, p9 & p30 (Chen Wei Seng), p10, p11 top (Freddy Eliasson), p11 bottom, pp12-13 (Jin Young Lee), p14 & p31 (Michel Stevelmans), p15 bottom (Gautier Willaume), p18 (Amy Nichole Harris), p19 top (Ke Wang), p19 bottom (Jarno Gonzalez Zarraonandia), p23 top (Velychko), p23 bottom (Kheng Guan Toh), p25 (Muellek Josef), p27, p28 top (Li Wa), p28 bottom (Bent G Nordeng), p29.

Cover photos: Shutterstock: main (Tomas Slavicek), left (sming), right (cupertino).

Printed in Singapore.

Franklin Watts is a division of Hachette Children's Books, an Hachette UK company.
www.hachette.co.uk

Contents

Off to China!

Today we are going to China.

China is a big country in the continent of Asia. It is divided into areas called **provinces**. The biggest province is Xinjiang.

500 kilometres

500 miles

RUSSIA

KAZAKHSTAN

MONGOLIA

KYRGYZSTAN

NORTH KOREA

JAPAN

TAJIKISTAN

Great Wall of China

SOUTH KOREA

Beijing

PAKISTAN

C H I N A

Xi'an

Nanjing

Shanghai

Yangtze River

Pacific Ocean

TAIWAN

NEPAL

BHUTAN

Hong Kong

INDIA

BANGLADESH

VIETNAM

PHILIPPINES

MYANMAR

LAOS

Here are some things I know about China...

- The **Great Wall** was built a long time ago. It is more than 8,800 kilometres (5,468 miles) long.
- There are many festivals in **China**. At some, a big colourful dragon is paraded through the streets.
- Most **Chinese** people eat using chopsticks.

On our trip I'm going to find out lots more!

China is so big that the **climate** changes from place to place. In the north it can be very cold. In the south it is often very hot.

We need to pack clothes for different types of weather.

Arriving in Beijing

We arrive in Beijing in the evening. Outside the airport it is hot and breezy.

We get on a bus that is going to the city centre. As we get closer to the city there are more and more buildings.

There are a lot of cars in Beijing. Mum says that this causes problems with **air pollution**.

There are also lots of people on bicycles.
Some people use them to travel to work.

Can you guess
how many bicycles
there are in China?

The answer is over
500 million.

Some bikes have
two wheels at the
back so that they
can carry heavy loads.

A day in Beijing

Today we are going to explore Beijing.
Beijing is the capital city of China.
Many people live and work here.

First we go to a park.
There are some
people dancing
with ribbons.
Others are doing **tai
chi.** Two old men are
playing Chinese chess.

At the park
Many Chinese cities
have big parks. People
spend a lot of free time
here, walking and meeting
friends. They do all sorts
of activities for fun
and exercise.

In the evening we go to see a Beijing opera. The characters are dressed in colourful costumes with brightly painted faces.

They sing in high voices. A man explains that the story is about a hero and a villain.

The Forbidden City

The next day we go to the Forbidden City. This was the palace of the emperors who ruled China a long time ago.

Inside the city there are lots of buildings. They are all painted in bright colours.

Did you know that in the Forbidden City there are 90 palaces and courtyards, 980 buildings and 8,704 rooms?

There are many statues in the city. My favourite is the tortoise statue.

When we leave the Forbidden City we cross over the road to a big, open square. This is Tiananmen Square.

In the evening we watch the flag-lowering ceremony. Soldiers march into the square. They lower the Chinese flag and fold it in a special way.

The Great Wall

Today we are going to see the Great Wall of China!

The wall was built hundreds of years ago to keep out invading tribes from other countries.

The wall is high up in the green hills. All along the wall are beacon towers.

When we get to the first tower, I look out of one of the old windows. The wall winds away as far as I can see.

Parts of the wall are very steep. We have to be careful not to trip on the broken stones.

Did you know that some of the towers have names? One is called the Fairy Tower. Another is called the Wangjinglou Tower. It is built on the highest part of the wall.

From Beijing we are going to go to Xi'an. This is another important city in China.

Beijing station is a huge building. There are lots of people with bags and suitcases.

Beijing station

We are going to travel to Xi'an on a sleeper train. In each **compartment** there are bunks to sleep on.

When we wake up we are nearly in Xi'an. Through the window we can see green hills and farmland. People are working in the fields. Now and then, we rush past villages.

Even though the cities are very busy, most people in China live in the countryside. Many of them are farmers. They grow **crops** and raise animals.

Rice plants

Different crops are grown in different places. Wheat is grown in the north and rice is grown in the south.

A Day in Xi'an

It is early morning when we arrive in Xi'an.

Long ago, China was ruled by **dynasties**. A dynasty is a family who rule one after the other. The head of the dynasty was the emperor. Many dynasties made Xi'an their capital city.

In the centre of the city is the Bell Tower. It is high up and we can walk underneath it. Nearby is the Drum Tower.

Bell Tower

Near the Drum Tower is Moslem Street. This is the best place to get snacks in Xi'an. We decide to try dumplings.

A dumpling is a round ball of pastry with a tasty filling. The filling might be fish, lamb, chicken or vegetables. There are sweet dumplings too, like these.

The terracotta warriors

Today we are going to see the terracotta warriors. The site is near the edge of the city so we travel there in a taxi.

Dad says that some farmers discovered the terracotta warriors. Over time, **archaeologists** have found over 7,000 warrior statues.

The statues were made for a Chinese emperor called Qin Shi Huang. He was the first emperor. He wanted the statues to guard his **tomb**.

The warriors look like a big army. The statues are the same size as real people.

They are all wearing armour and there are horse statues too.

Did you know that the Emperor Qin Shi Huang started building his tomb when he came to power at the age of thirteen? It took more than 30 years to build.

In Nanjing

From Xi'an we take a train to a city called Nanjing. When we leave the station a group of school children walk past.

A school day
For children in China school usually starts at 8 o'clock in the morning. Before lessons they do exercises. They go home for lunch and then have more lessons in the afternoon.

Most signs in China are written in Chinese characters as well as letters, like the ones in this book. Chinese characters look like symbols. Altogether there are over 40,000 of them!

In one shop we see a man writing Chinese characters. He uses a brush with a long, soft tip and black ink.

A f--mily me--l

In the evening we go for a meal. There are lots of families eating in the restaurant. Parents, children and grandparents are all eating together.

How many children?

Most Chinese families have just one child. The population in China is growing very quickly so the government tells families not to have too many children.

In the restaurant everyone is eating with chopsticks. These are sticks that you use to pick up food. It is quite tricky. We each have a little bowl and spoon to use too.

First, we order soup with lots of different things in. Next, we have a dish of roast duck, some vegetable dishes and rice. All the food is placed in the middle of the table so we can share it. I like the roast duck best.

Roast duck

At the market

Before we leave Nanjing we go to the market. There are people everywhere. The stallholders call out to us to buy things.

Some stalls are piled high with fruit and vegetables. There are lots of types I have not seen before.

Other stalls are selling fish. The smell is very strong.

We all buy presents for friends and souvenirs to take home.

Mum buys tea. I buy a purse made of silk and a model of a golden cat that is supposed to be lucky.

Lucky golden cat

Tea is grown all over China. People in China believe that tea is very good for you. At traditional tea drinking ceremonies you can learn about different types of tea.

Along the Yangtze River

From Nanjing we are going to Shanghai. We will travel by boat along the Yangtze River. The journey will take ten hours!

The Yangtze River is very important. It provides lots of water for farmland. Many farmers grow crops on the land near the Yangtze River.

Lots of boats are using the river. Some carry people. Others carry **cargo**. Cargo could be anything, from coal to toys.

When we reach Shanghai the river becomes very wide and there are many other boats. There are lots of big buildings in Shanghai. My favourite is the Oriental Pearl Tower.

Oriental Pearl Tower

Did you know that the Chinese name for the Yangtze River is Chang Jiang? This means 'long river'. The Yangtze is the longest river in China.

Exploring Hong Kong

From Shanghai we fly to Hong Kong.

In Hong Kong, we take the **tram** to the top of Victoria Peak. From here we can see the whole city.

Dad shows us a map of Hong Kong. It is a large area that includes part of the **mainland** and lots of islands.

In the city we see modern skyscrapers. Some are so tall we cannot see the tops. Then we go to a busy market. It smells of spices and fish.

In the evening we go to Victoria Harbour for our last meal in China. All the tall buildings are brightly lit. When we get back to our hotel, we will have to pack our bags for the flight home tomorrow.

I found out that Hong Kong was ruled by the British government for a long time, from 1898 until 1997.

Ni Hao (*say* **Nee how**)	Hello
Zai jian (*say* **Tz-eye jan**)	Goodbye
Ni Hao Ma (*say* **Nee how mah**)	How are you?
Xie Xie (*say* **Shee-eh shee-eh**)	Thank you
Ni jiao shen mee ming zi? (*say* **Nee jee-ow shen ma ming zee**)	What is your name?
Wo jiao Sarah. (*say* **Wo jee-ow Sarah**)	My name is Sarah.

Counting 1-10

1 **yi** 2 **er** 3 **san** 4 **si** 5 **wu**

6 **liu** 7 **qi** 8 **ba** 9 **jiu** 10 **shi**

air pollution when air is made unclean by chemicals or other substances

archaeologist a scientist who learns about the past by digging up old objects and buildings and examining them

cargo goods that are carried by a boat or plane

climate the usual weather in one place

compartment a small room in a railway carriage

crop plants that are grown for food

dynasty the family of rulers of a country

mainland the main part of a country, not the islands

province a region of a country

tai chi a Chinese form of physical exercise involving movements and meditation

tomb a grave for an important person

tram a vehicle that carries passengers. A tram runs on rails.

Index

Learning more about China

Books

China (Arts and Crafts of the Ancient World) Ting Morris, Franklin Watts, 2006.
China (Festivals of the World) Colin Cheong, Franklin Watts, 2006.
China (Food Around the World) Polly Goodman, Wayland, 2010.
China (Looking at Countries) Jillian Powell, Franklin Watts, 2006.

Websites

National Geographic Kids, People and places
  http://kids.nationalgeographic.com/places/find/china
Geography for kids, Geography online and Geography games
  http://www.kidsgeo.com/index.php
SuperKids Geography directory, lots of sites to help with geography learning.
  http://www.super-kids.com/geography.html

Been There!

Join us on an amazing trip to CHINA!

Travel with us by plane, boat and train, to learn about China, its countryside and towns. We'll see how people live, and sample different types of food. We'll explore the Great Wall, see the famous terracotta warriors and visit bustling Hong Kong.

The **Been There** series explores countries through a 'travel diary', with all the excitement of a real visit, and provides historical and geographical information. Come with us as we journey to some of the most exciting countries in the world.

Special features include:
- A country Fact File.
- Full colour map showing our route around the country.
- Fascinating fact boxes.
- Some first words in the main language of the country.

Titles in the series:

Been There! BRAZIL — 9781445132860

Been There! CHINA — 9781445132853

Been There! FRANCE — 9781445132877

Been There! INDIA — 9781445132884

Been There! ITALY — 9781445132891

Been There! MEXICO — 9781445132907

Been There! SOUTH AFRICA — 9781445132914

Been There! SPAIN — 9781445132921

FRANKLIN WATTS

£8.99

ISBN 978-1-4451-3285-3
9 781445 132853
www.franklinwatts.co.uk